Seb Jarnot

3 x 7 = 15

To Fred and Lou.

When he was at school, Seb Jarnot's parents ran a bar in the small French town of Doué la Fontaine and were busy most of the time. Like his brother and sister, Seb was quite free to do what he liked. During this period two essential events occurred that play an important role in the making of this book.

First of all, one of the bar's customers, who knew that Seb was interested in images, gave him his collection of French "Photo" magazines from the mid 1970s to early 80s. This was Seb's first encounter with artists such as Richard Avedon, Brassaï, Helmut Newton, Joel-Peter Witkin, Larry Clark, Mary Ellen Mark and many more. There were many strange photo reportages on topics including eroticism, war, suicide, India, junkies and gay life in New York City. Seb was around 13 years old at the time ("maybe a bit too young," he recalls) and was fascinated by those eclectic and bizarre pictures. He began drawing a lot of the images that he saw in those magazines.

Secondly and at around the same time, Seb was a fan of three French caricaturists named Mulatier, Ricord and Morchoine who created a series of books called "Les grandes gueules" (literally "the big gobs"). In one of these books Seb found one of their birthdays. He wrote to him for the occasion and sent him some drawings. A few days later he got an encouraging postcard back from the caricaturist, which concluded with the words "...and maybe see you later in the profession". Seb says getting that postcard made him happier than he has ever been in his whole life except at his daughter's birth. He even slept with it for an entire week and, because hearing from the artist meant so much to him, he still has the postcard.

These two little anecdotes help a bit in understanding Seb Jarnot's artistic background. He has also found inspiration in Picasso and Modigliani, and later in Renoir, Toulouse Lautrec, Ingre, Rubens and Rembrandt. Although, like a lot of illustrators, he admits to being more inspired by bizarre music acts than visual artists.

His contemporary influences include Japanese illustrators such as Yoshimoto Nara, but most of all he's attracted to the covers of Japanese, American and French comics. He deeply admires Robert Crumb, whose work also led him to Raymond Pettibon. Seb has been and still is fascinated by their dynamic, strange and often very "attractive" approach. Still, it's worthwhile to take a closer look at his own genuine style.

In order to learn more about Seb's approach, I think it is necessary to understand that France and Belgium are definitely the strongholds of European comics culture. While most of its popular creations (such as Asterix, the Smurfs and TinTin) are well known to a mainstream market, there is also an intimidating output of lesser known high quality adult graphic novels and illustrations from Tardi and Nicolas de Crécy to Marseilles' "Le Dernier Cri" editions to mention only a few. Seb Jarnot's illustrations should be seen in the context of this subculture. To me, the one word that best describes Seb's work is "fantastic". Practically every drawing has a kind of surreal approach and creates a supernatural atmosphere. This is especially extraordinary given that his favourite implement is the ballpoint pen, a tool that makes giving personal expression to the line it creates rather difficult. In contrast to the variations that a calligrapher can create by applying changing pressure to a brush, it is next to impossible to vary the width and intensity of a line made by a ballpoint. To me, what a ballpoint pen represents is the contradiction of "fantastic".

The fantastic approach is supported by the way Seb draws faces. A lot of them seem blurred or smeared; they have no eyes at all or an overstock of them, like spiders. While the rest of his people seem to look quite normal, their faces resemble insects or aliens or a monster from a Jack Arnold pulp movie. But upon closer examination, the same very simple lines define several perspectives or expressions of the same person. In this way, Seb's lines are far from being simple and are among the most elaborate linear constructions I know. Whenever he uses brushes to create his lines, they incorporate sheer dynamism and, with one simple stroke, express the sheer beauty of movement and form itself.

In Seb Jarnot's illustrations you can find the lightness of someone who draws so much and so passionately that all of this lightness seems to come naturally, without the use of force or any obvious effort. I hope you enjoy discovering his work for yourself.

Robert Klanten, dgv

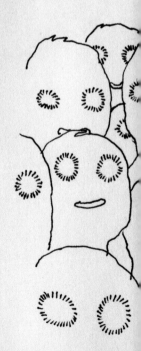

STÚ

K ON GUM

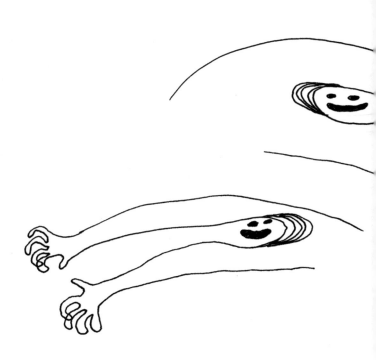

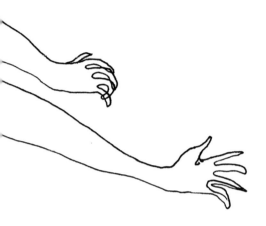

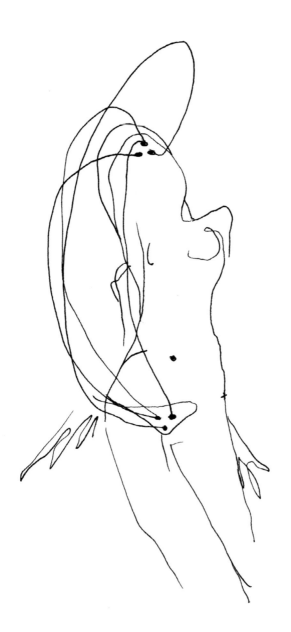

15

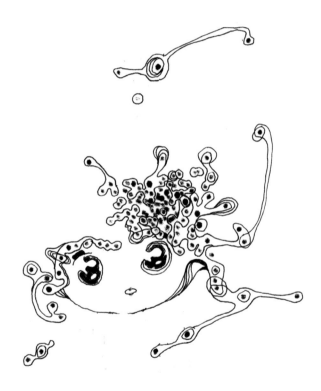

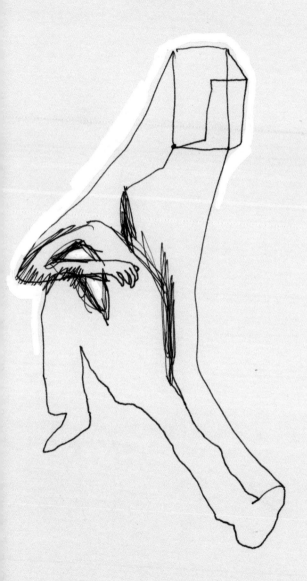

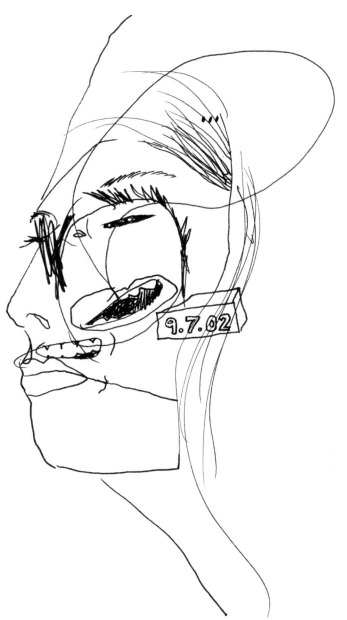

cont~~~~
continuous
mode

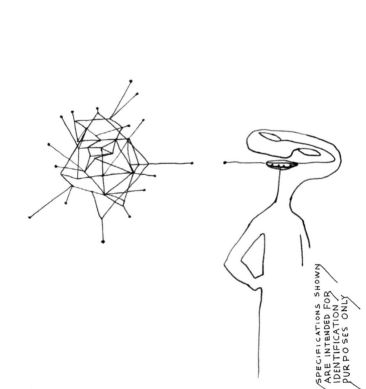

SPECIFICATIONS SHOWN
ARE INTENDED FOR
IDENTIFICATION
PURPOSES ONLY

SCI FI SEX

AUTOÉGOPORTRAITCENTRIQUE

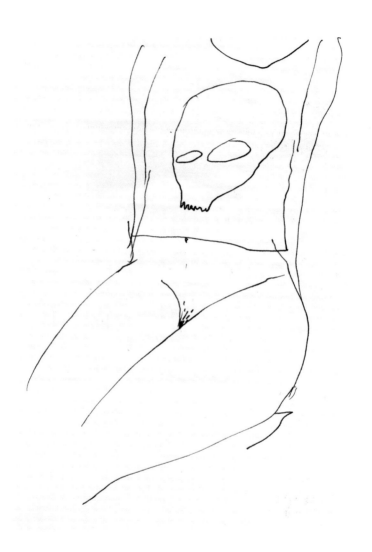

30

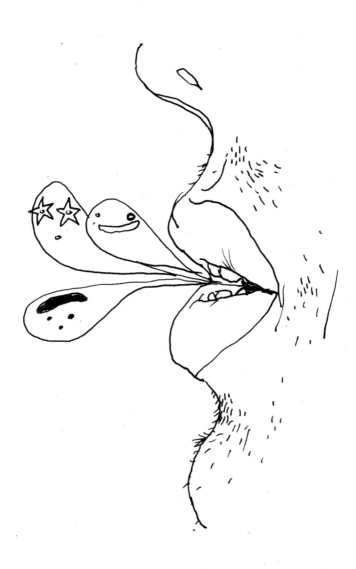

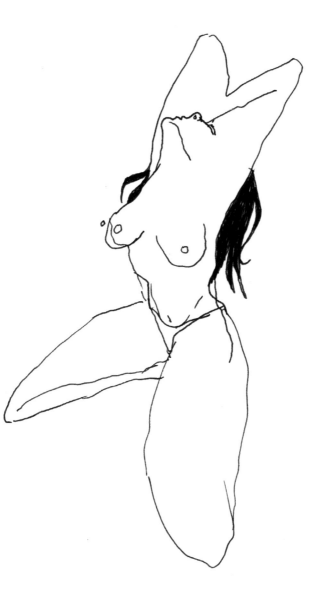

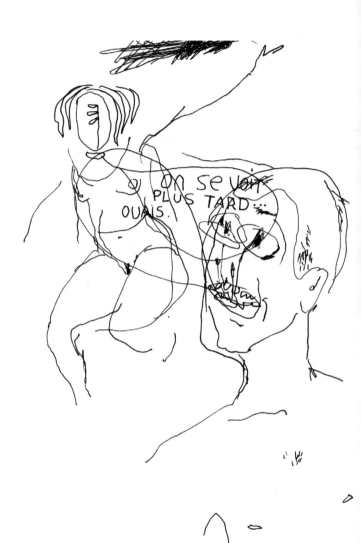

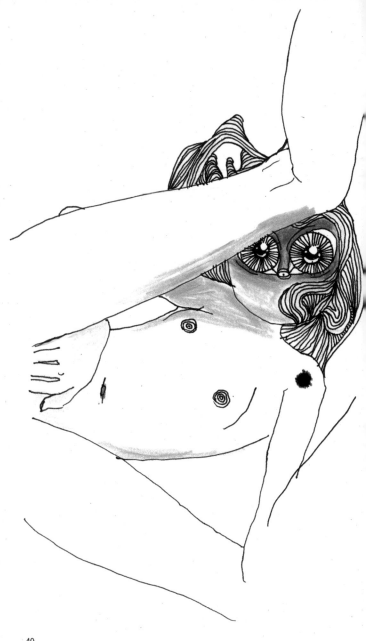

La jeune fille et le joint

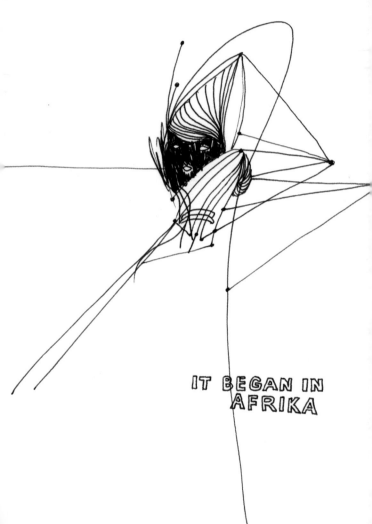

IT BEGAN IN
AFRIKA

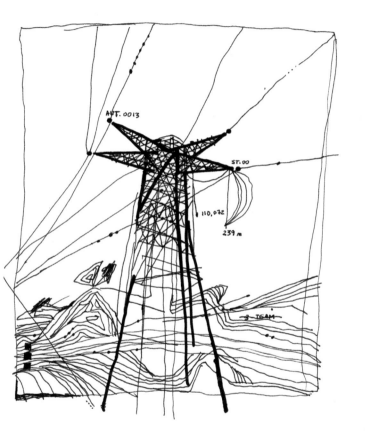

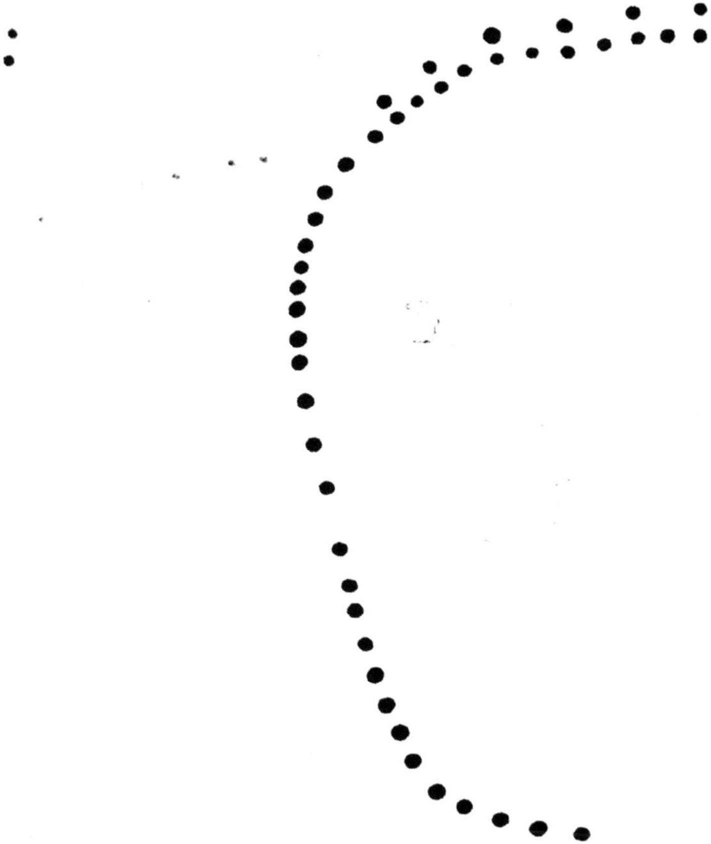

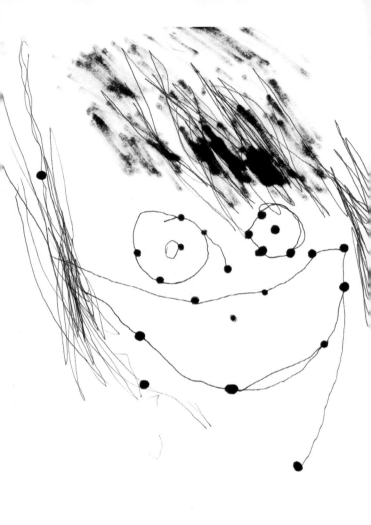

(with a bit of drama)

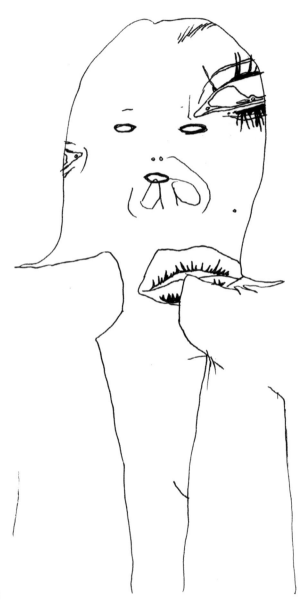

EGE + FRED
/12/01

59

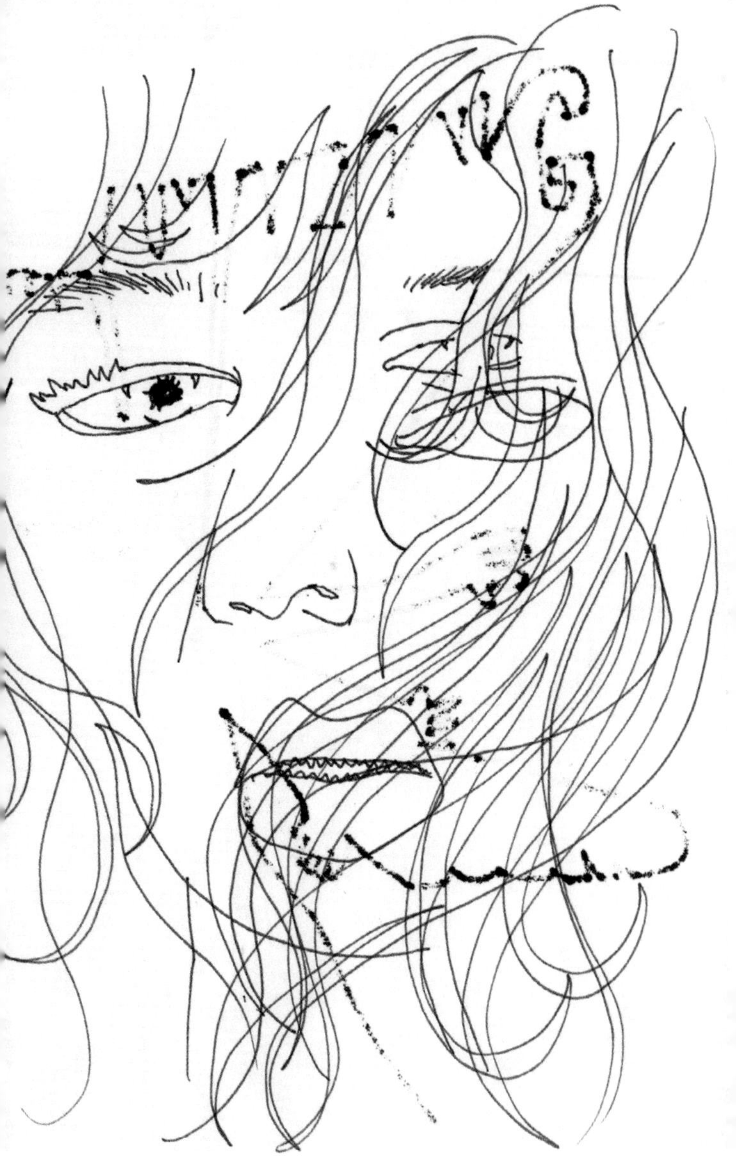

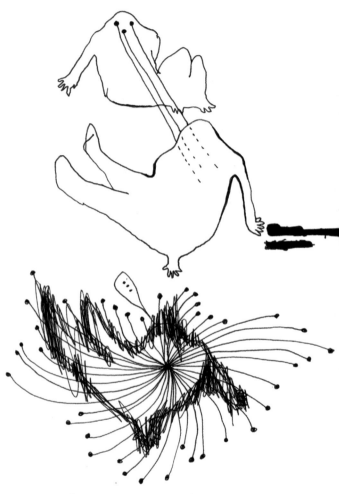

- DÉMATÉRIALISATION SPONTANÉE -

30 7

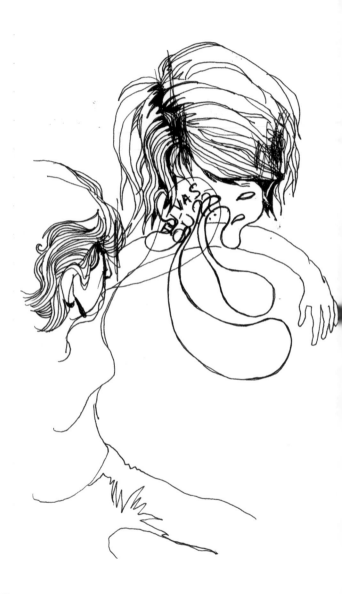

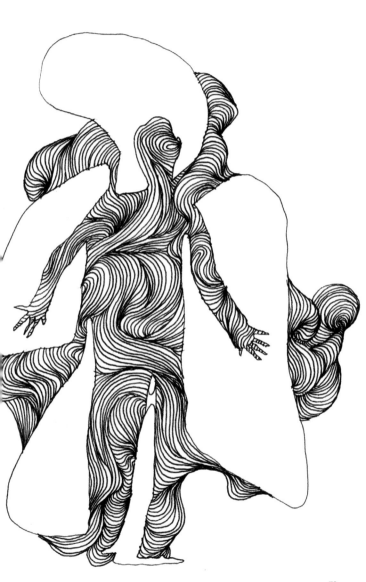

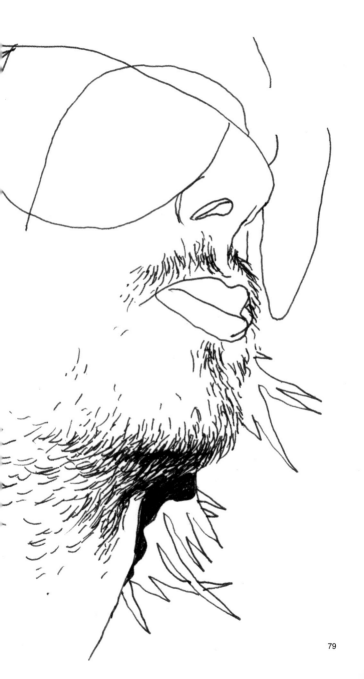

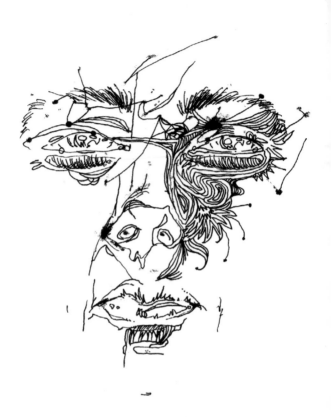

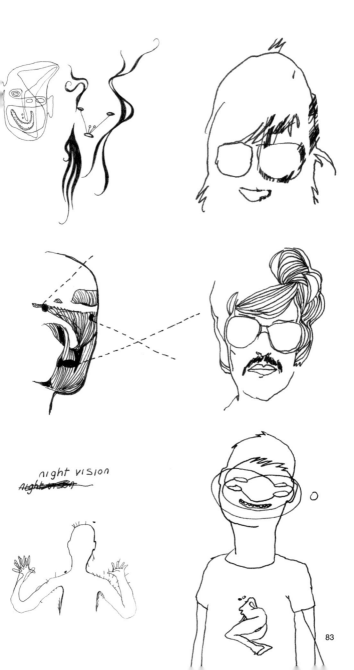

night vision

83

The man with the red face
Laurent Garnier

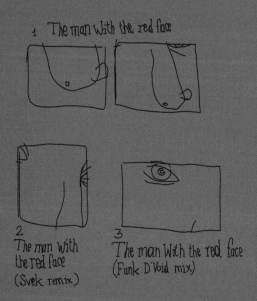

1 The man with the red face

2
The man with
the red face
(Svek remix)

3
The man with the red face
(Funk D'Void mix)

Laurent
Garnier
Unreasonable li

F 155 DVD 137.0155. 077/425°
CMV 5 0155 77 137/ACX

Laurent
Garnier
Unreasonable behaviour

Laurent Garnier "Unreasonable behaviour" (album), 2002 F Communications

Laurent Garnier

greed + the man with the red face

(part (part two)
one)

A-1 greed (Fabrice Lig mix) 5'52"
A-2 greed (Dave Clarke mix) 5'40"
AA-1 the man with the red face 8'05"
A-2 greed (part one) 5'58"
(Ashley Beedle mix) A-2 greed (April mix) 6'20"
AA-1 the man with the red face
(Llorca Driver mix) 6'27"

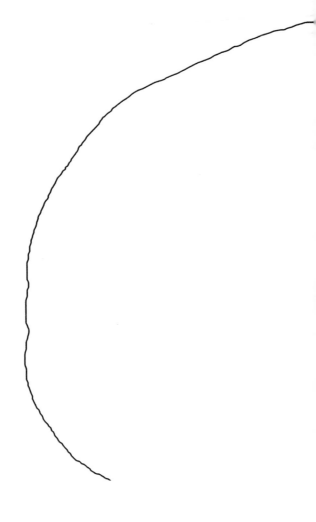

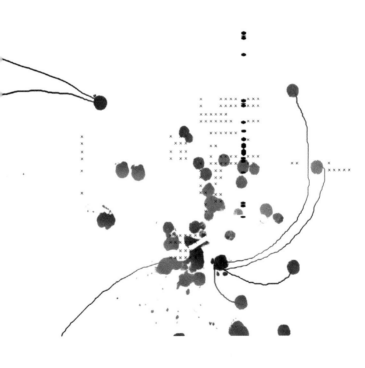

Novanov
Memor

electronic with no limit

communications

artwork / rob jarnot

Exhibition flyer for V.I.A. 2003

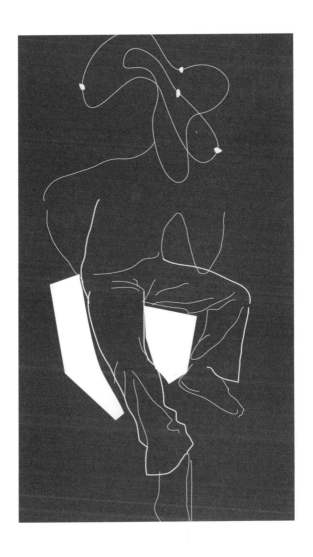

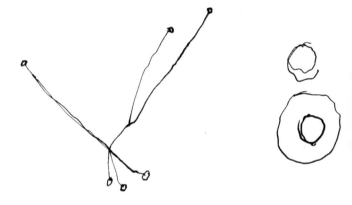

The Youngsters "Smile remixes" (CD), 2002 F Communications

1 (03:40) SMILE → PROFIL'S MIX (EDIT)
2 (08:45) GIVING THE HOUSE TO THE SPACE CHILD
3 (06:12) SMILE → SMIRKY MIX

WRITTEN, PRODUCED AND MIXED
BY THE YOUNGSTERS
IN (MONTPELLIER :)

WWW.THEYOUNGSTERS.NET

ORIGINAL VERSION FROM "LEMONORANGE" ALBUM F144CD
MASTERING BY TOP MASTER   DESIGN BY SEBJARNOT

MADE IN GERMANY

CMV 6054 27137/CD SABAM/BIEM (LC) 01547
℗ 2002 F COMMUNICATIONS
© 2002 F COMMUNICATIONS BY PIAS BENELUX
RELEASED UNDER LICENSE IN PIAS GERMANY AND CREATIVE VIBES, AUSTRALIA
DISTRIBUTION IN FRANCE BY PIAS FRANCE UK BY CHARGED/VITAL
GERMANY BY CONNECTED, AUSTRALIA BY CREATIVE VIBES, SPAIN BY MASTERTRAX

F COMMUNICATIONS → 20/22 RUE RICHER 75009 PARIS
INFO@FCOM.FR
WWW.FCOM.FR
Ⓕ

ELECTRONIC
WITH NO LIMIT

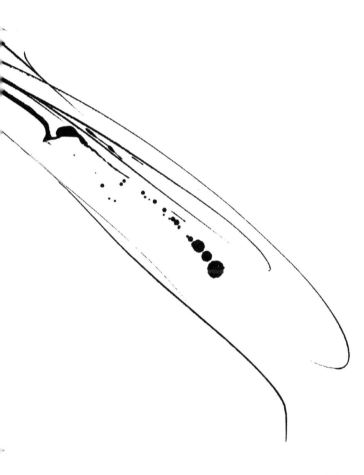

NERU TANK
KARATI CAPRI

Nike Print Campaign, Apparels Spring/Summer 2002, see credits p. 192

COMPONENTS FLEECE CREW
PEACH POPLIN PANT

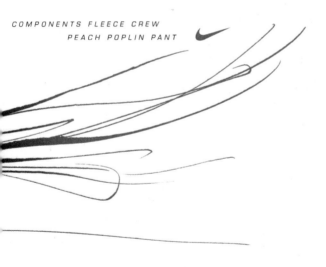

EXT. OUTDOOR VENTED JACKL
STMNT. OUTDOOR

DRIVING JACKET
FOUNDATION PANT

TRAINING TANK
BUDO PANT

LLORCA WITH LADY BIRD MY PRECIOUS THING

LLORCA WITH NICOLE GRAHAM INDIGO BLUES

LLORCA
NEW
COMER

LIFE IS TOO SHORT TO MISS HIS FIRST EXPLORATION OF HOUSE AND FUNK...

AVAILABLE IN CD & VYNIL Ⓕ

"French Polar", published in Up Street 2001

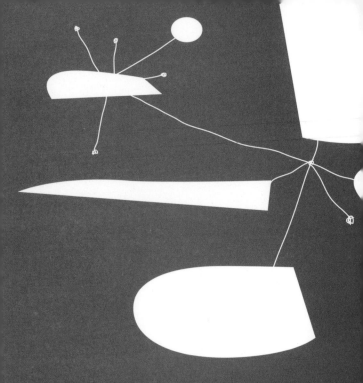

"Mobiles", published in Double, 2000

133

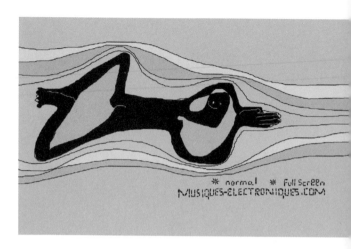

Fictitious ad published in "Margeting", a book by André Platteel (NL), 2003

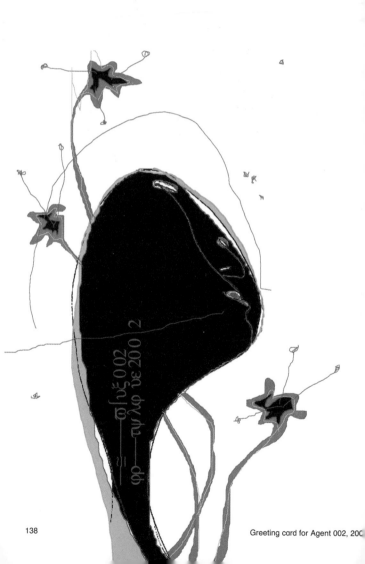

3×7= 15   205

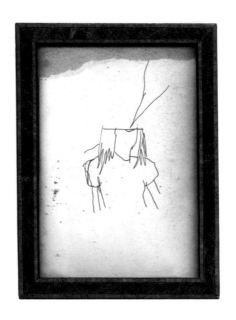

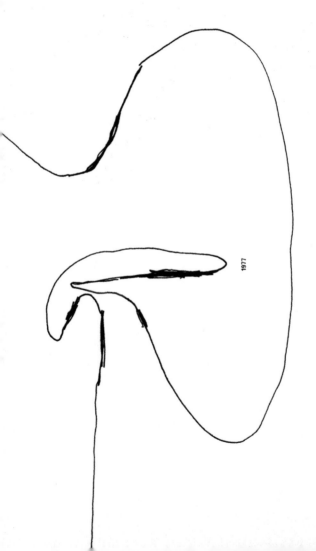

1977

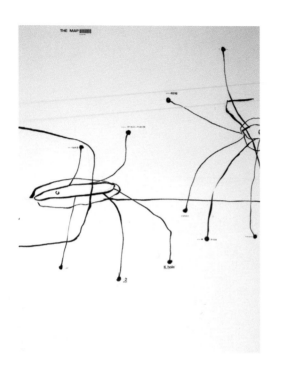

K. hole

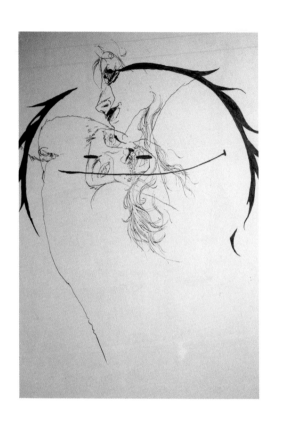

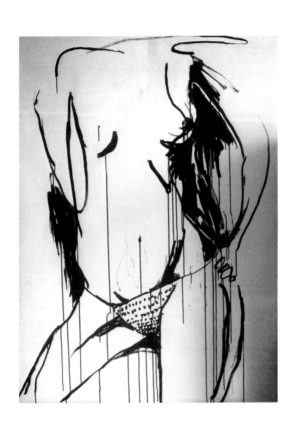

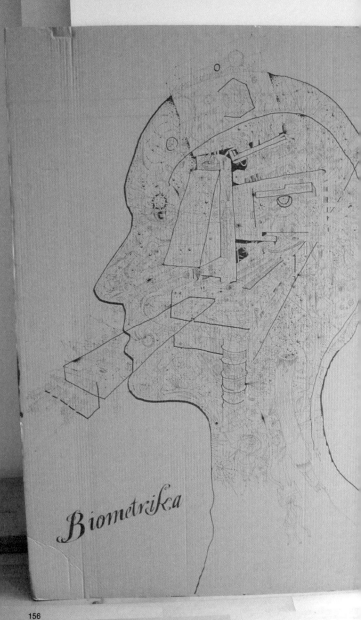

Biometrika

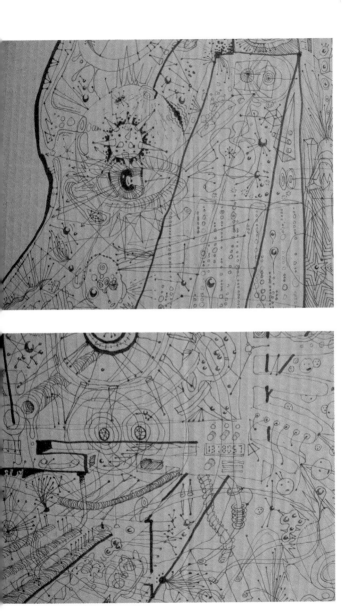

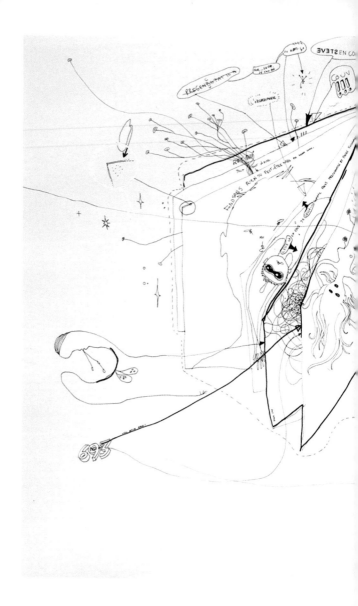

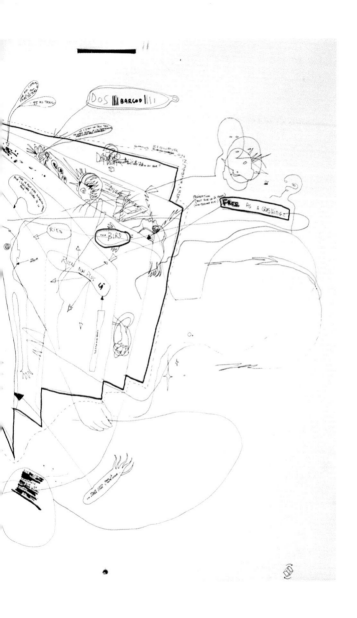

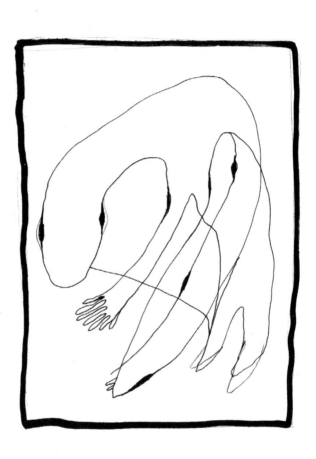

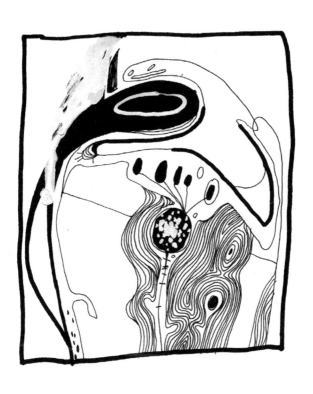

9 02 03   1:27

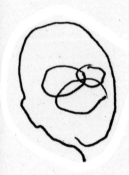

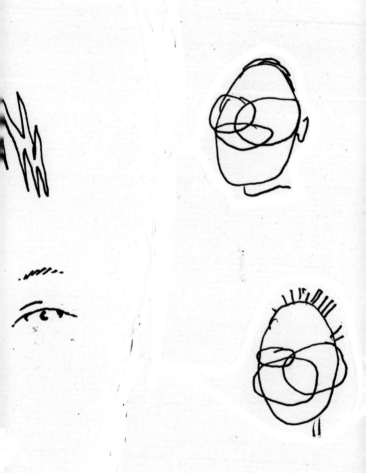

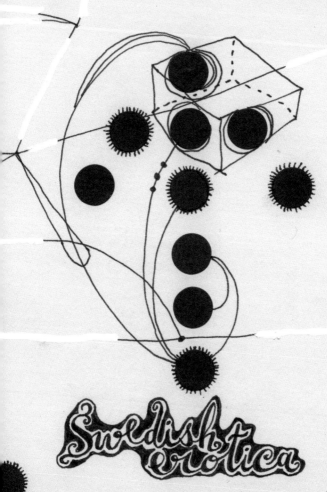

BEACH (Le grau du roi)

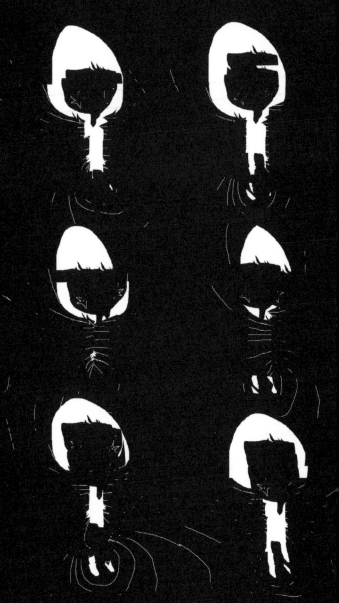

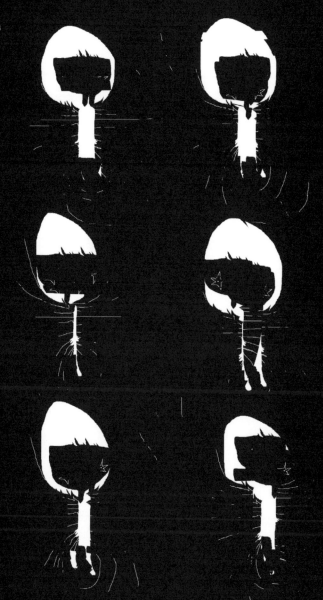

(덧미)

Shouts to all friends and family for their love and support.

Thanks to Robert Klanten, Hendrik Hellige, Janni Milstrey and Sven Ehmann, without whom this book would have not been possible. Special thanks to Eric Dalbin, Philippe Pannetier, Eric Morand and everybody @ Fcom.

Seb Jarnot $3 \times 7 = 15$

Edited by Robert Klanten and Hendrik Hellige
Production Management: Janni Milstrey

Made in Europe.

Bibliographic information published by Die Deutsche Bibliothek. Die Deutsche Bibliothek lists this publication in the Deutsche Nationalbibliografie; detailed bibliographic data is available in the Internet at http://dnb.ddb.de.

ISBN 3-89955-057-9   © dgv – Die Gestalten Verlag, Berlin 2004

Credits for Nike Print Campaign, Apparels Spring / Summer 2002 > Agency: Wieden + Kennedy (NL / Amsterdam) • CD: Paul Shearer / Glenn Cole • AD: Merete Busk • SA: Janine Byrne • PJM / PDM: Nicola Applegate • AE: Gemma Requesens • AB: Tracy Kelly • Photos: Alan Clarke • Illustrations: Seb Jarnot • Color Tag Creative: Frazer Goodbody • Country: International

Credits for Nike Print Campaign, Apparels Fall / Winter 2002 > Agency: Wieden + Kennedy (NL / Amsterdam) • CD: Paul Shearer / Glenn Cole • AD: Merete Busk • SA: Janine Byrne • PJM / PDM: Nicola Applegate • AE: KayHoffman • AB: Tracy Kelly • Photos: Juan Algarin • Illustrations: Seb Jarnot • Color Tag Creative: Frazer Goodbody • Country: International